After You

By Janine Amos   Illustrated by Annabel Spenceley

Gareth Stevens Publishing
A WORLD ALMANAC EDUCATION GROUP COMPANY

Please visit our web site at: www.garethstevens.com
For a free color catalog describing Gareth Stevens'
list of high-quality books and multimedia programs,
call 1-800-542-2595 (USA) or 1-800-461-9120 (Canada).
Gareth Stevens Publishing's Fax: (414) 332-3567.

Library of Congress Cataloging-in-Publication Data

Amos, Janine.
    After you / by Janine Amos; illustrated by Annabel Spenceley.
        p. cm. — (Courteous kids)
    Includes bibliographical references.
    ISBN 0-8368-2802-X (lib. bdg.)
    1. Courtesy—Juvenile literature. [1. Etiquette. 2. Conduct
of life.] I. Spenceley, Annabel, ill. II. Title.
BJ1533.C9A46   2001
395.1'22—dc21   00-049293

This edition first published in 2001 by
Gareth Stevens Publishing
A World Almanac Education Group Company
330 West Olive Street, Suite 100
Milwaukee, WI 53212 USA

Gareth Stevens editor: Anne Miller
Cover design: Joel Bucaro

This edition © 2001 by Gareth Stevens, Inc. First published by Cherrytree Press,
a subsidiary of Evans Brothers Limited. © 1999 by Cherrytree (a member of the
Evans Group of Publishers), 2A Portman Mansions, Chiltern Street, London
W1M 1LE, United Kingdom. This U.S. edition published under license from
Evans Brothers Limited. Additional end matter © 2001 by Gareth Stevens, Inc.

Printed in the United States of America

1 2 3 4 5 6 7 8 9 05 04 03 02 01

Going to the Park

Raúl, Tyler, and Jamal are going to the park.

They are in a hurry to start playing ball.

The boys get to the park gate.

So does Mrs. King.
The gate is narrow.

Tyler and Jamal push through the
gate at the same time as Mrs. King.

Her baby stroller gets stuck.
How does Mrs. King feel?

Raúl waits and lets Mrs. King go first.

How does Mrs. King feel now?

Raúl catches up with his friends.

Jesse and Max

Jesse and Max are painting.

14

They both try to wash their
brushes at the same time.

The water spills.

The paintings are ruined.

Jesse and Max start again.

Jesse needs to wash his brush,
but first, he thinks about it.

19

This time, Jesse lets Max go first.

Mr. Potter

Shannon and LaSheka go to the store.

They want ice cream. The shop is busy.

Mr. Potter is next in line.

But two older girls take his turn.

How does Mr. Potter feel?

LaSheka and Shannon walk up to the counter.
They see Mr. Potter ahead of them.

The girls think about Mr. Potter.
They wait for him to go first.

How does Mr. Potter feel now?

More Books to Read

Manners. Aliki (Greenwillow)

Me First. Helen Lester (Houghton Mifflin Co.)

Oops! Excuse Me Please!: And Other Mannerly Tales.
Bob McGrath (Barrons Juveniles)

Perfect Pigs: An Introduction to Manners. Marc Brown &
Stephen Krensky (Little, Brown & Co.)

Note to Parents and Teachers

The questions that appear in **boldface** type can be used to initiate discussion with your children or class. Encourage them to think of possible answers before continuing with the story.

Additional Resources

Parents and teachers may find these materials useful in discussing manners with children:

Video: *Manners Can Be Fun!* (ETI-KIDS, Ltd.)
This video includes a teacher's guide.

Web Site: *Preschoolers Today: Where Have the Manners Gone?*
www.preschoolerstoday.com/resources/articles/manners.htm